Illustrated by STACY HELLER BUDNICK

I Am
Why Two Little Words Mean So Much

From the *New York Times* best-selling authors . . .

DR. WAYNE W. DYER

with Kristina Tracy

HAY HOUSE, INC.
Carlsbad, California • New York City
London • Sydney • New Delhi

Published in the United States by: Hay House, Inc.: www.hayhouse.com
Published in Australia by: Hay House Australia Pty. Ltd.: www.hayhouse.com.au
Published in the United Kingdom by: Hay House UK, Ltd.: www.hayhouse.co.uk
Published in India by: Hay House Publishers India: www.hayhouse.co.in

Cover design: Julie Davison • *Interior design, and editorial assistance:* Jenny Richards • *Illustrations:* © Stacy Heller Budnick

Library of Congress Control Number of the original edition: 2011944404

Hardcover ISBN: 978-1-4019-6218-0
E-Book ISBN: 978-1-4019-6250-0

10 9 8 7 6 5 4 3 2 1
1st edition, March 2012
2nd edition, May 2021
Printed in the United States of America

Dear Parents and Teachers,

I am so excited to share this new book with you and your children. My studies and teachings over the past several years have led me to write a book for adults called *Wishes Fulfilled*. I have taken the most important concept from *Wishes Fulfilled* and created this children's book. The concept is that God is not separate from us but is actually an energy living inside of us. Once we become aware of this energy, we can help it to grow and expand and bring happiness to ourselves and others. What I hope to offer children with this book is the understanding that they are a part of God and God is a part of them. I like to explain it like this: Imagine God as the ocean. If you take a bucket of water out of the ocean, is it still the ocean? Yes! God is the ocean, and we are the buckets of water drawn from the ocean—separate, but one.

I named this book *I Am* because of the incredibly powerful meaning of those two words. How we finish the sentence that begins with "I am" makes all the difference in the life we create for ourselves and how close or far away we are from the part of us that is God. I have included more on the use of "I am" at the end of the book. My wish is that each one of us comes to recognize and connect to the amazing gift that is God's love.

Dr. Wayne W. Dyer

Hello, my friend—
　　do you know who I am?

Listen carefully to this
　　rhyme, and try to
　　　　guess if you can!

Do I live in the clouds
so far away?

Or is a temple or a church
the place that I stay?

I am in those places,
yes, that is true,
But only because I am in you.

We are not separate—
wherever you are, I am there.
I am in your mind and your heart . . .
I am everywhere!

You're like a candle lit
     from my bright flame.

My light is your light—
     we are one and the same.

I am everything that is good
and everything that is real,
I am the source of
all the warmth you feel.

I am the part of you that shares and gives from your heart.

I am **the inspiration** behind your music, sports, and art.

I am the voice that you hear
when you are quiet and still,
I am the little bird
on your windowsill.

I am in everyone you see—
young or old, big or small,
Believe it or not,
I am in them all.

Who can I be? I AM GOD, your best friend.

And there's really no line

where you start and I end.

Did you hear what I said—**are you listening?**
For you will be amazed at what this
knowledge will bring.

You will live your life knowing it is never just you,
and that **we are together**
in all that you do.

Along the way,
you will find
great happiness
and love,

And you'll learn that
wishes come true
from within,
not above.

So, don't look to the sky
        when you're looking for me,
Look right at **yourself** . . .
        and that's where I'll be!

The Meaning of "I Am"

As you read this book, you may have noticed that many of the sentences start with the words *I am*. These are two of the most powerful words you can use to begin a sentence. The important thing is what words you use to finish that sentence. Anytime you start a sentence with *I am*, you are creating what you are and what you want to be. At the same time, you are also showing whether or not you are connected to the energy of God inside of you. So, if you sometimes say, "I am bad at this, I am ugly, I am stupid," these words take you farther and farther away from the part of you that is God. When you choose to say, "I am happy, I am kind, I am perfect," you help the light of God inside you to grow and shine. Try saying some *I am* sentences. See how different words make you feel.

I am_____

I am_____

I am_____

I am_____

I am_____

We hope you enjoyed this Hay House book. If you'd like to receive our online catalog featuring additional information on Hay House books and products, or if you'd like to find out more about the Hay Foundation, please contact:

Hay House, Inc., P.O. Box 5100, Carlsbad, CA 92018-5100
(760) 431-7695 or (800) 654-5126
(760) 431-6948 (fax) or (800) 650-5115 (fax)
www.hayhouse.com® • www.hayfoundation.org

Published in Australia by: Hay House Australia Pty. Ltd.,
18/36 Ralph St., Alexandria NSW 2015
Phone: 612-9669-4299 • Fax: 612-9669-4144
www.hayhouse.com.au

Published in the United Kingdom by: Hay House UK, Ltd.,
The Sixth Floor, Watson House, 54 Baker Street, London W1U 7BU
Phone: +44 (0)20 3927 7290 • Fax: +44 (0)20 3927 7291
www.hayhouse.co.uk

Published in India by: Hay House Publishers India,
Muskaan Complex, Plot No. 3, B-2, Vasant Kunj, New Delhi 110 070
Phone: 91-11-4176-1620 • Fax: 91-11-4176-1630
www.hayhouse.co.in

**Access New Knowledge.
Anytime. Anywhere.**

Learn and evolve at your own pace with the world's leading experts.

www.hayhouseU.com